Where We Live

Sweden

Donna Bailey

RSVP

RAINTREE
STECK-VAUGHN
PUBLISHERS

Hello! My name is Lars.

I live in the city of Stockholm.

Stockholm is the capital of Sweden.

Stockholm is on the edge of the Baltic Sea
where an inlet from the sea joins Lake Mälaren.
Part of the city is on the mainland and
part of it is built on islands, so
there are many waterways in the city.

There are many islands in Lake Mälaren and
in the Baltic Sea outside the capital.
Many people from Stockholm spend
their weekends and vacations
in summer homes on the islands.

People go to the islands by ferry
from Stockholm.
Some of the ferry boats leave from
near Town Hall.

People also enjoy sailing boats
around the islands.
During the summer there are many
regattas and races.
People take picnics and watch the races.

Stockholm is a busy, modern port.
Ferries take passengers and cars from
Stockholm to other parts of Sweden or
to other countries.
Cruise ships dock at the wharf.

Downtown Stockholm has many big shops
and modern buildings.
Tourists like to buy Swedish glass
and jewelry as souvenirs.

Our home is in the suburbs of Stockholm,
away from the city center.
Our house is painted bright yellow.
We have big trees and flowering bushes
in our yard.

My school is not far from our house.
School starts at 8:15 every morning.
In the summer, I ride my bike to school
with my friends.

In Sweden we have two school terms.
The autumn term is from August
to December.
The spring term is from January
to June.

After school, my friends and I go to
a recreation center near the school.
We play games and learn crafts.
I go home at about 5:00 when Mom and
Dad get home from work.

In the winter, we go skating after school.
Lake Mälaren freezes up and people skate for
miles along the coast or from island to island.

The temperature drops so low in winter
that people must drill holes through the ice,
if they want to catch the fish in the lake.

During winter vacation, I go to a ski school
in the mountains.
We learn cross-country skiing.
At the end of the course, we have
cross-country races.

On summer weekends, we like to watch
the chess players in the Kungsträdgården,
a park in the center of Stockholm.
The players have to walk across the board
to move their giant chess pieces.

16

Sometimes we take a picnic lunch and
visit the Skansen Museum.
The Skansen is an outdoor museum with
houses from different parts of Sweden.
The houses and exhibits show
scenes from Swedish history.

During the Swedish summer, days
are long and nights are short.
Many people leave the cities and
go to Dalarna to stay
in a summer home.

18

People spend a lot of time
swimming, sailing, and canoeing.

The summer visitors enjoy
fishing in the lakes.
Many people like to barbecue the fish
and eat outdoors.

20

Everyone in Sweden looks forward to
the Midsummer Festival at the end of June
when summer days are the longest.
During midsummer, people have special races.
They race their decorated boats to church.

Before the festival, children pick flowers
and use them to decorate homes,
cars, and churches.

On the morning of the festival, children
weave garlands of flowers.
Even the youngest girls wear garlands
in their hair.

Every village has a maypole in the shape
of a cross.
People decorate the maypole with flowers and leaves.
In the afternoon, everyone gathers
to watch the raising of the maypole.

Once the maypole is raised, musicians
tune their instruments and play
traditional tunes and dances.

Many people wear their traditional costumes
and dance their favorite Swedish dances
around the maypole.

Parents teach their children the steps
of the dances.
Young and old join hands and
dance together.

Children who have learned the steps at
school perform while their family
and friends watch.

The fun and dancing go on until late at night.
Children are allowed to stay up
until the sun rises at about
2:00 in the morning.

Another popular holiday is the festival
of Saint Lucia on December 13.
Every office, school, and club chooses a Lucia.
She wears a white gown and a crown of
candles in her hair.

Each Lucia has a train of attendants.
The girls wear flower garlands and the boys
wear tall, pointed hats with golden stars on them.
As they walk through the streets, the children sing
traditional Lucia carols.

People wait in darkness for Lucia to appear.
After singing the carols, the children give
their parents and teachers ginger cakes
and saffron buns.

Index

Editorial Consultant: Donna Bailey
Executive Editor: Elizabeth Strauss
Project Editor: Becky Ward

Picture research by Jennifer Garratt
Designed by Richard Garratt Design

Photographs
Cover: Eija Haukio
A Shot in the Dark Photo Library: 2, 6, 11, 13, 14, 19, 22, 26, 27, 29
Susan Griggs Agency: title page (Michael Boys), 8 (John Heseltine), 10, 23, 28 (R. Rowan),
    15, 21 (Ted Spiegel)
Tom Hanley: 31
Robert Harding Picture Library: 9, 12, 16, 25, 32
Spectrum Colour Library: 17, 20
Swedish National Tourist Office: 24, 30
Zefa: 3, 4, 5, 7, 18

Library of Congress Cataloging-in-Publication Data: Bailey, Donna. Sweden/written by Donna Bailey.
p. cm.—(Where we live) Includes index. Summary: Describes life in the Swedish capital of Stockholm, on
the edge of the Baltic Sea. ISBN 0-8114-2567-5 1. Sweden—Social life and customs—Juvenile literature.
2. Stockholm (Sweden)—Social life and customs—Juvenile literature. [1. Sweden—Social life and customs.
2. Stockholm (Sweden)—Social life and customs.]
I. Title. II. Series: Bailey, Donna. Where we live. DL631.B285   1991   948.7′3—dc20   91-22052   CIP   AC

ISBN 0-8114-2567-5
Copyright 1992 Steck-Vaughn Company
Original copyright Heinemann Children's Reference 1991

3 4 5 6 7 8 9   LB   01   00   99